Hello Everyone,

Welcome to my adult coloring book, "Flower Garden Fantasy"! I have hand illustrated you 40 beautiful flower garden patterns. There is a variety of fun and challenging designs to color. Some of the patterns are more complex than others. I have included a test page so you can test out your pencils, crayons or whatever medium you choose.

Thank you for purchasing my adult coloring book!

I would like to thank the best boyfriend in the world, Brian Dages for his support! xoxo

Suzanne Lapila - Illustrator - Author

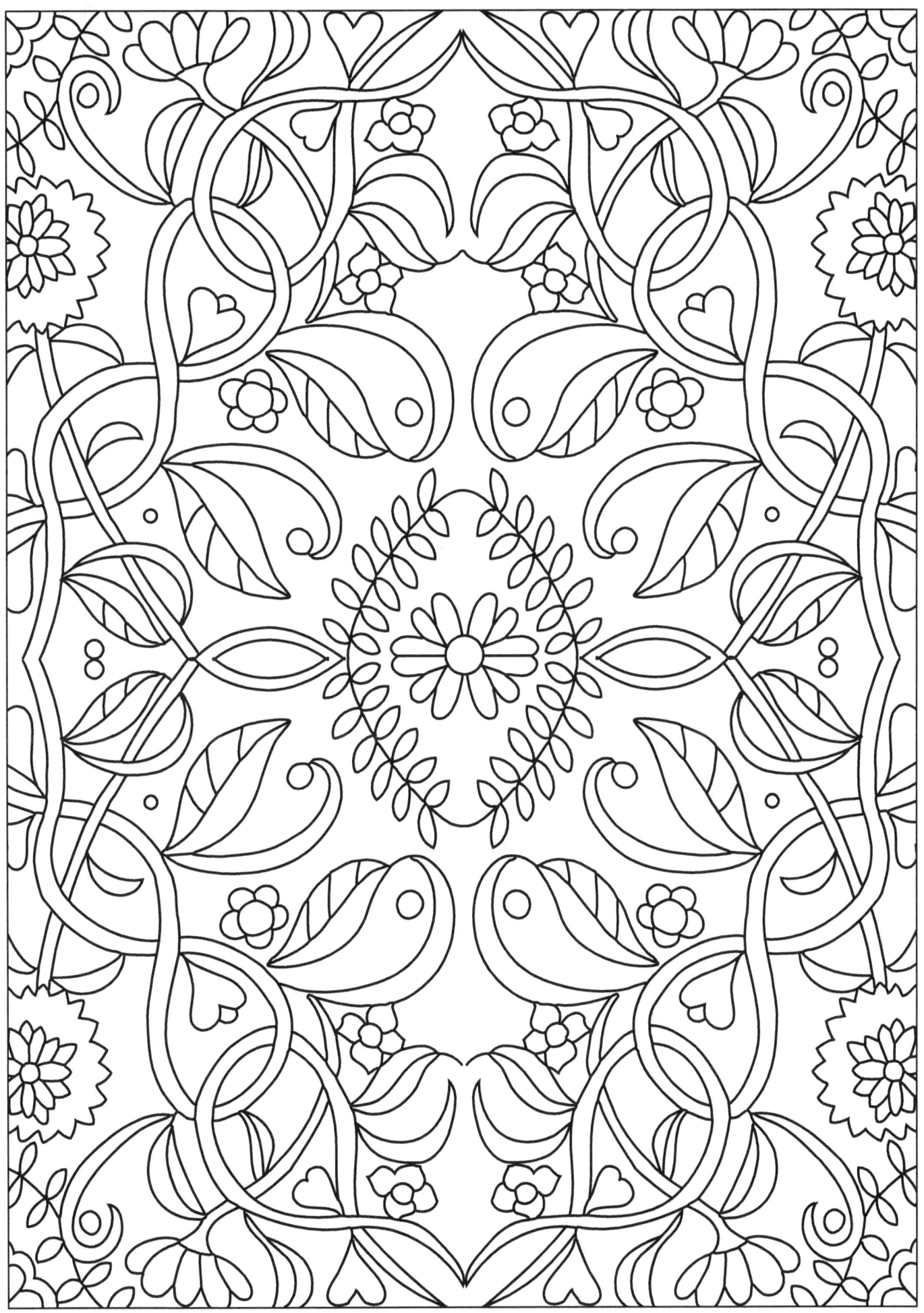

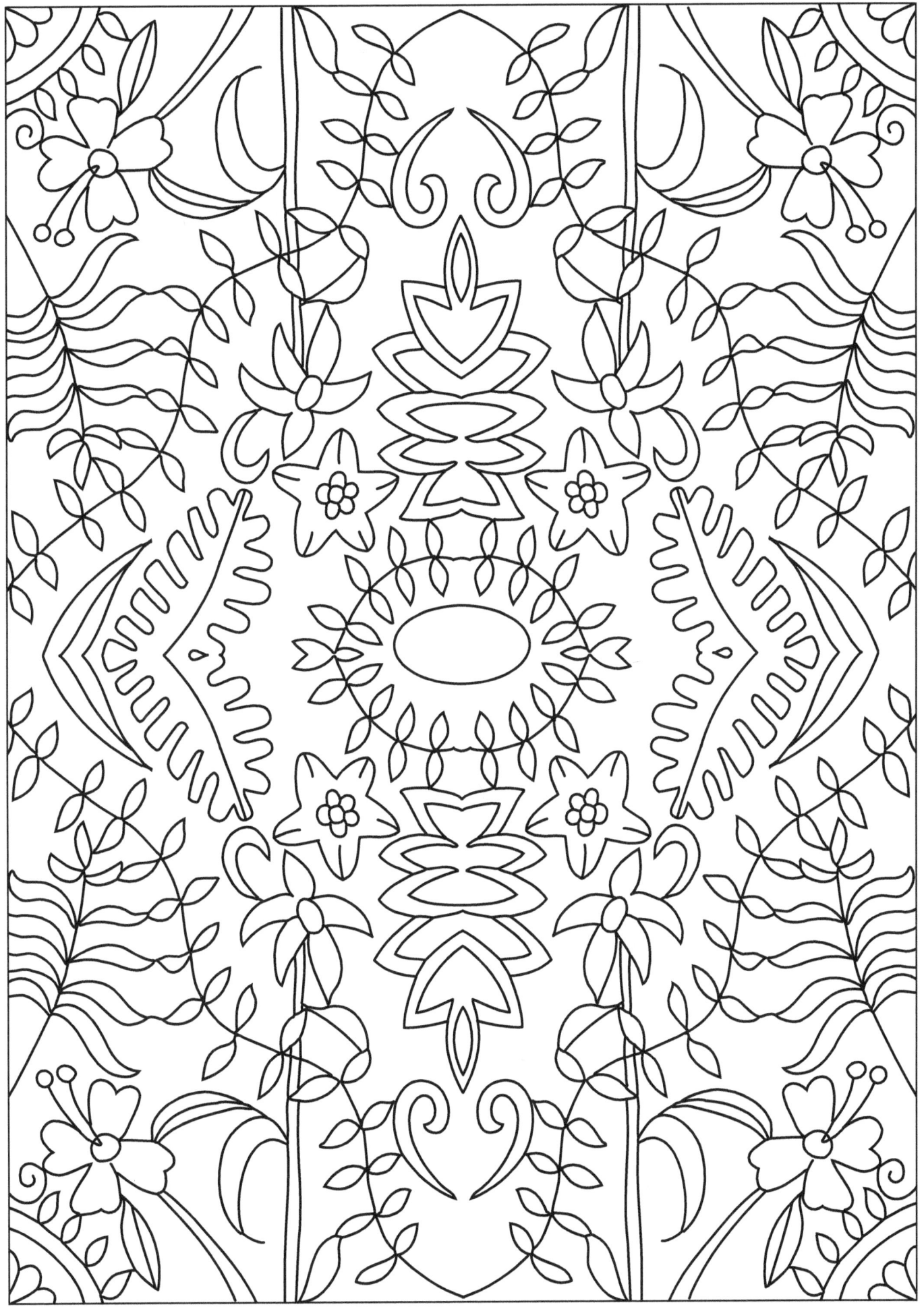

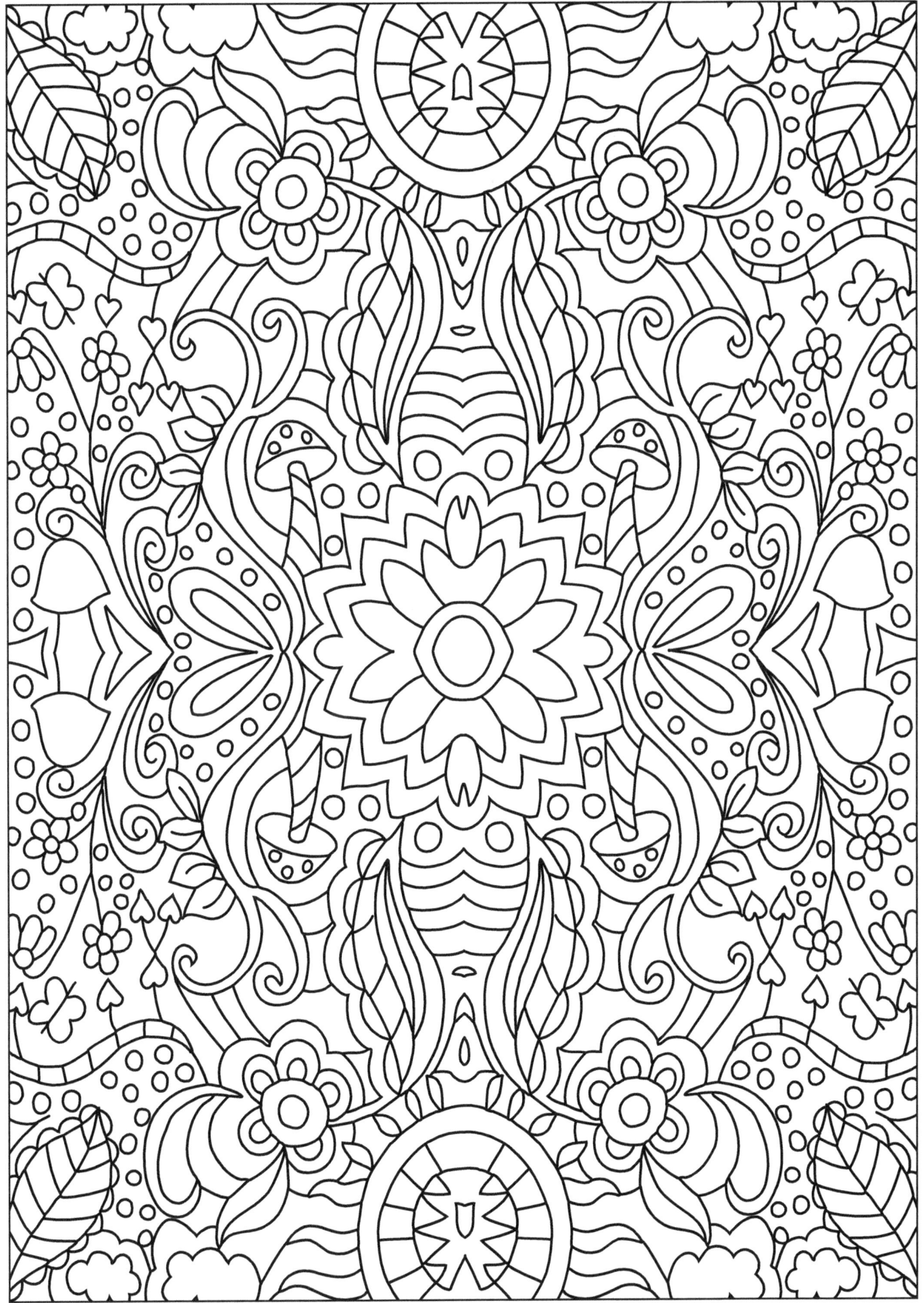

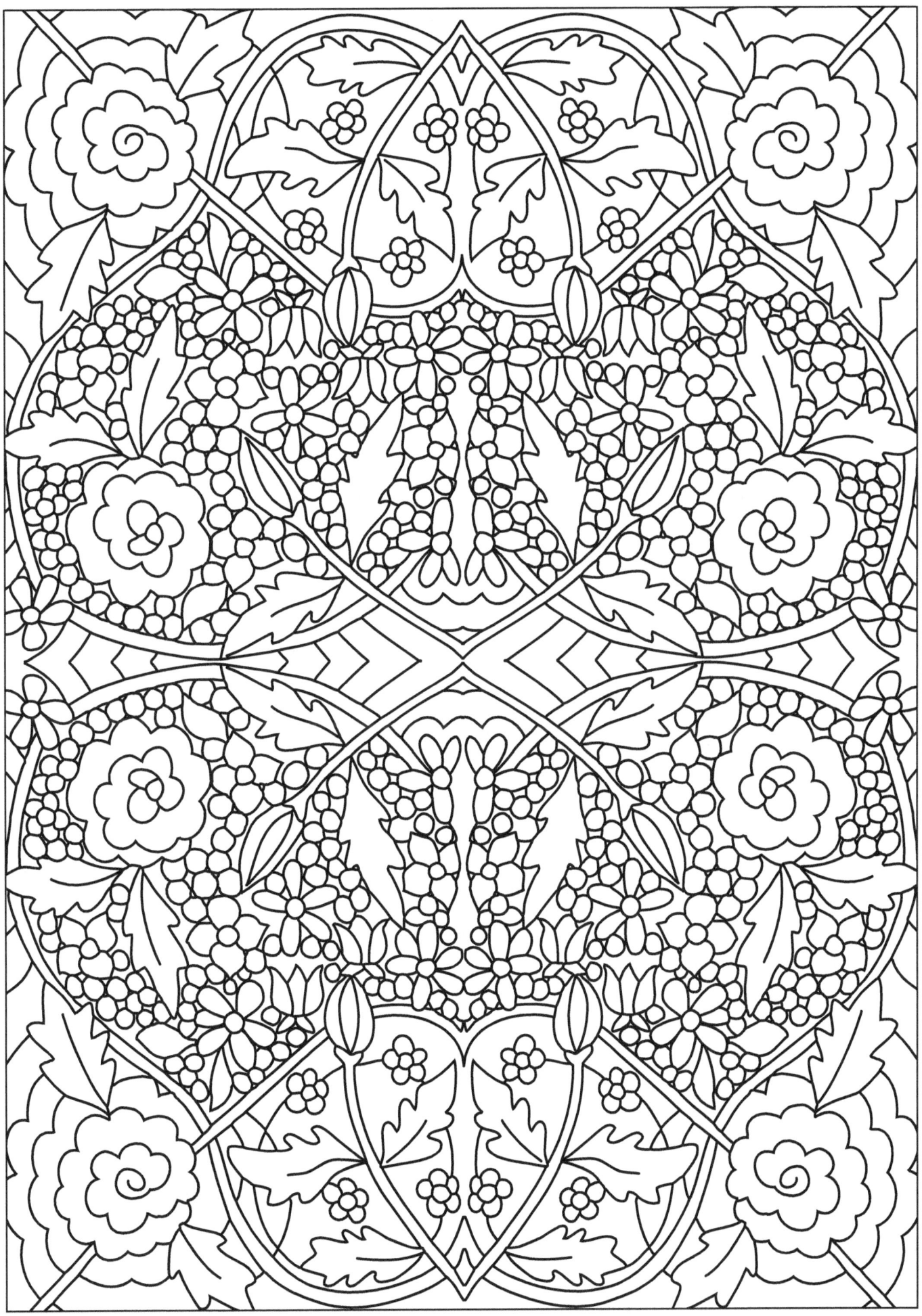

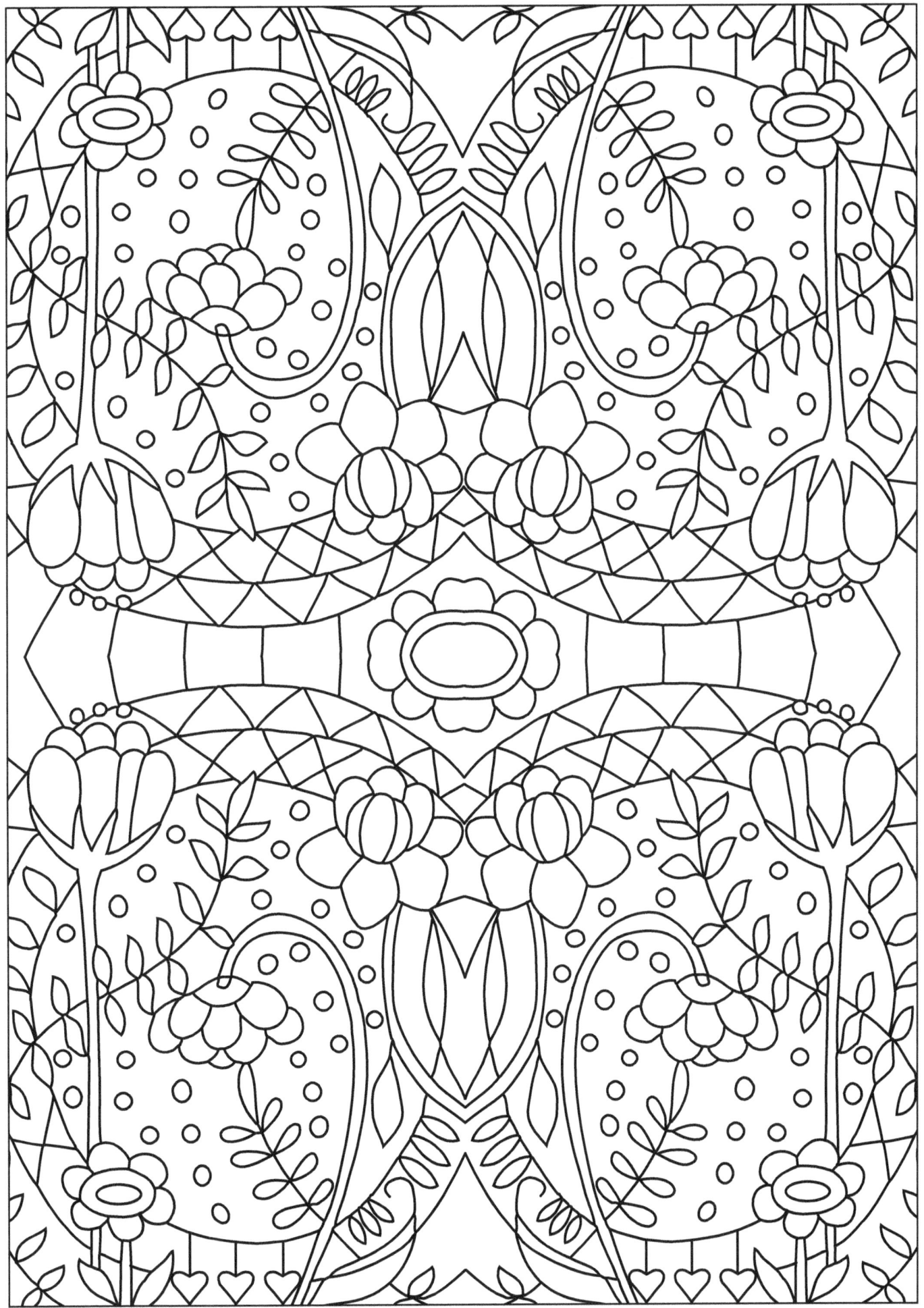

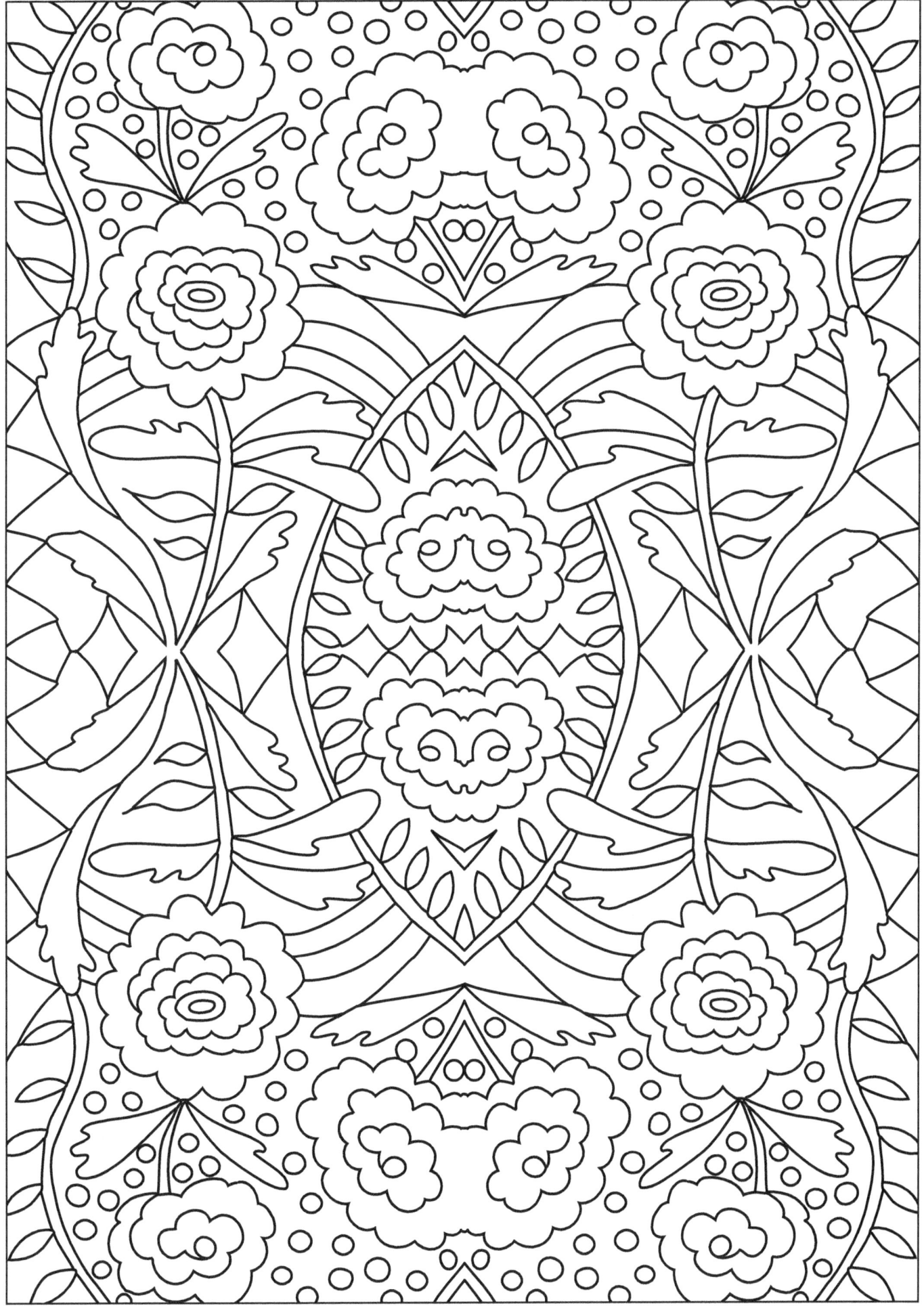

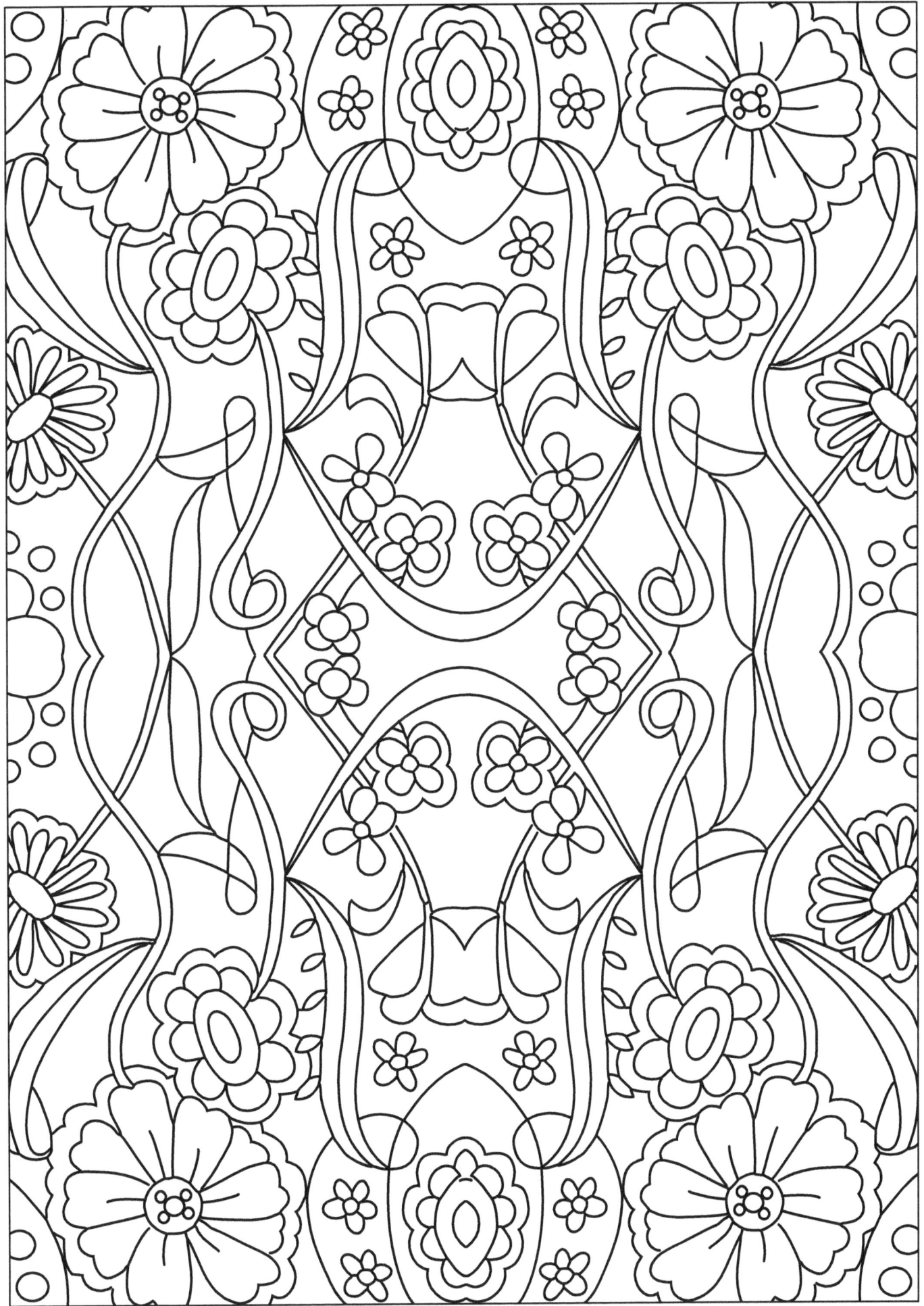

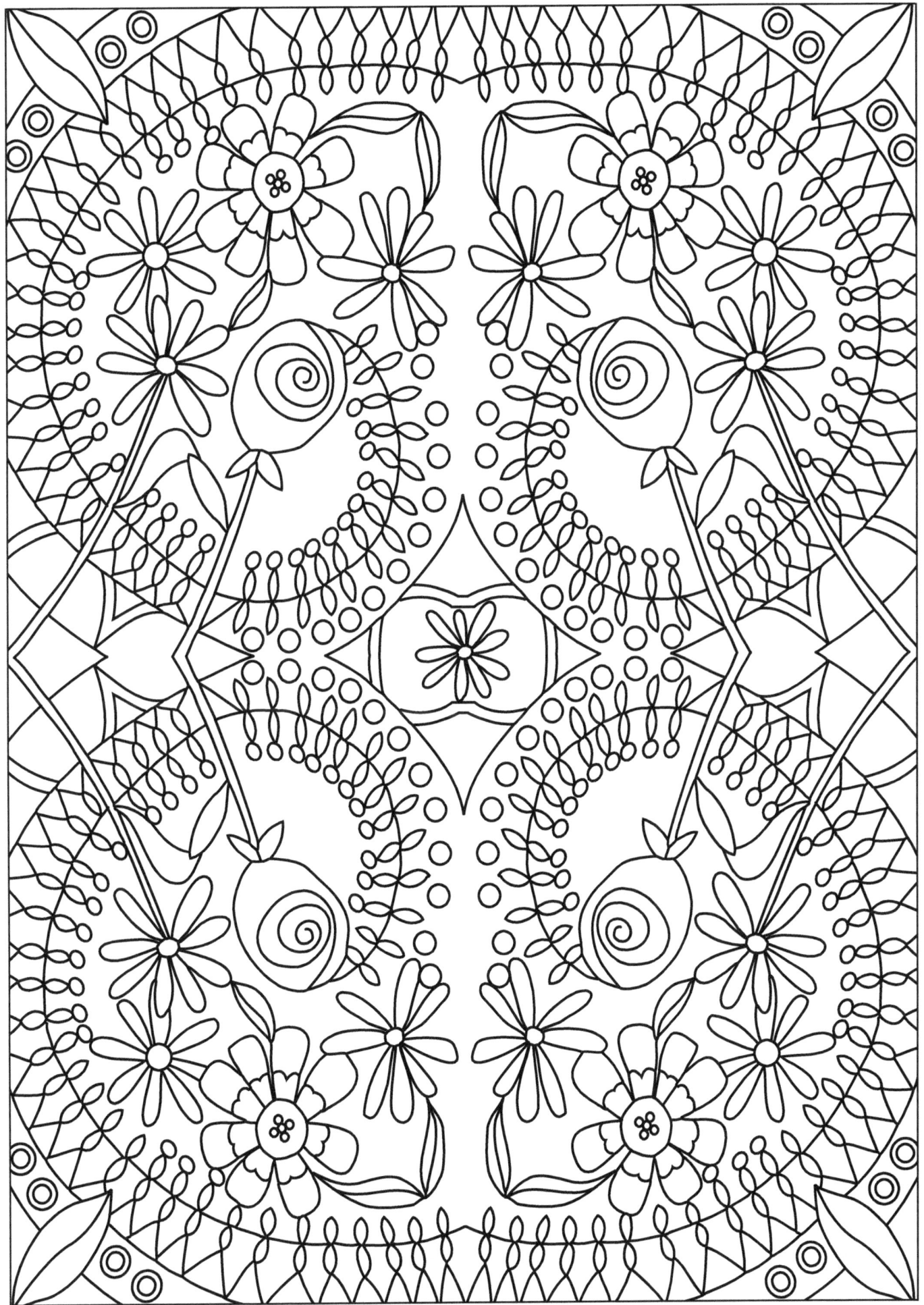

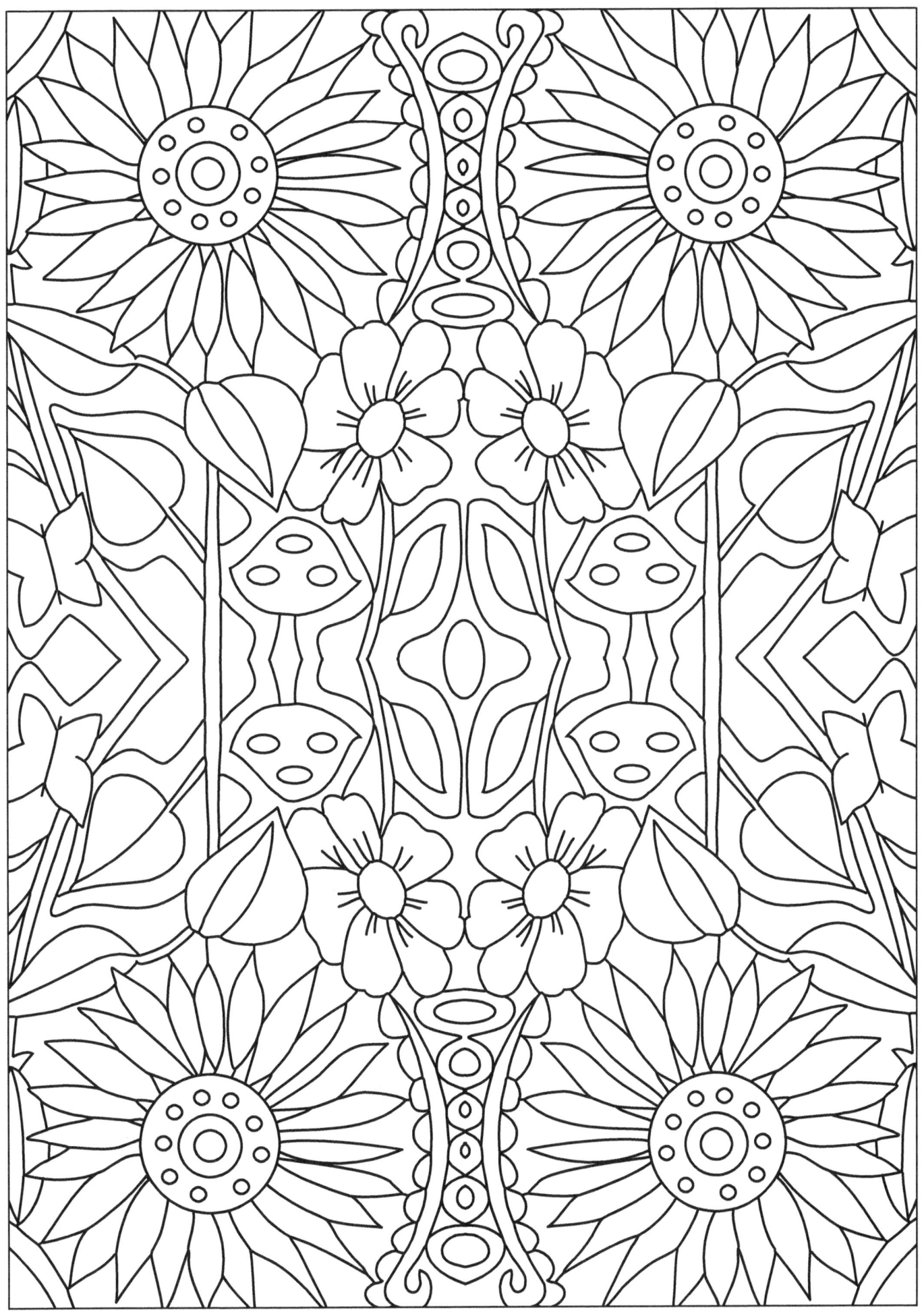

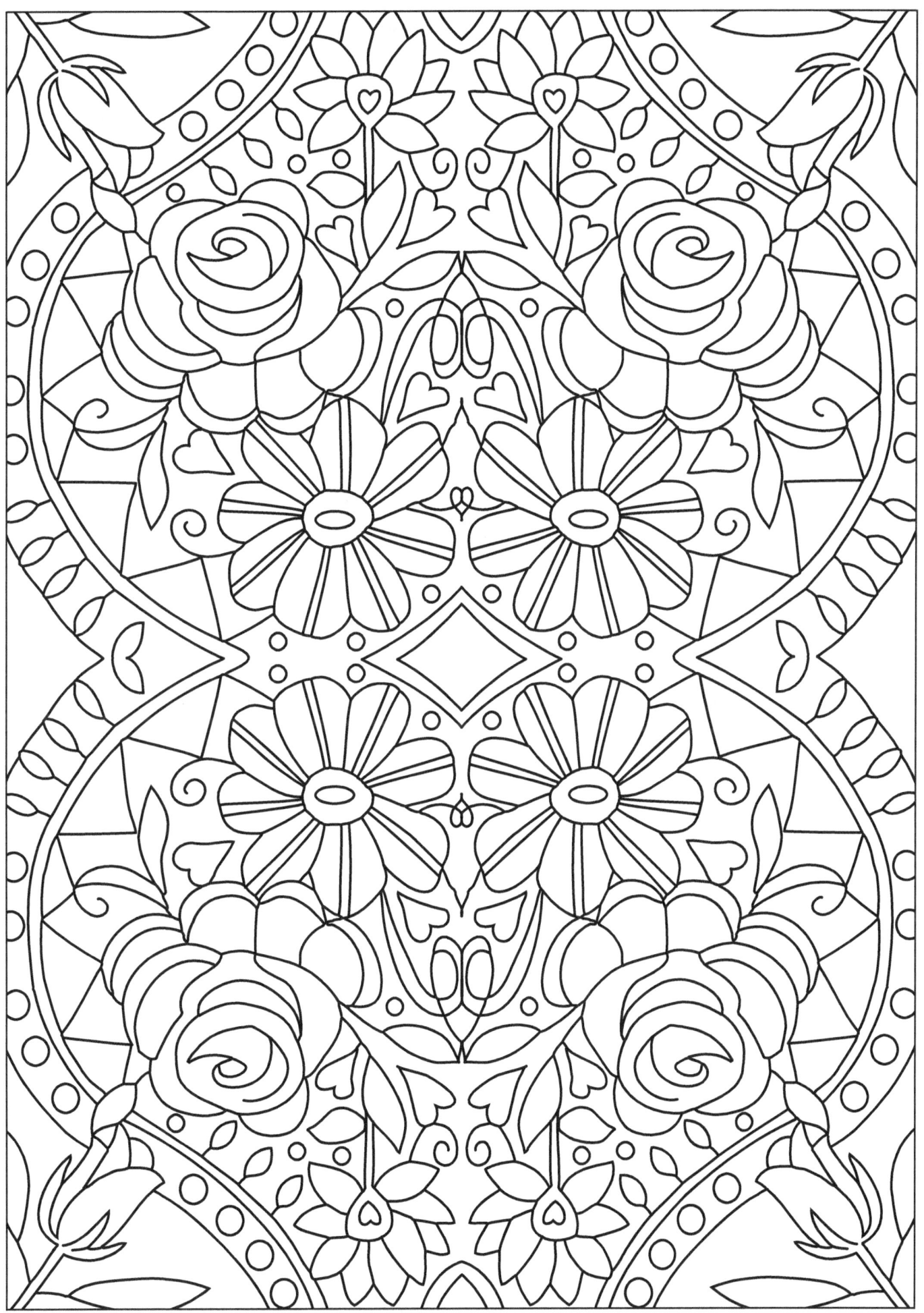

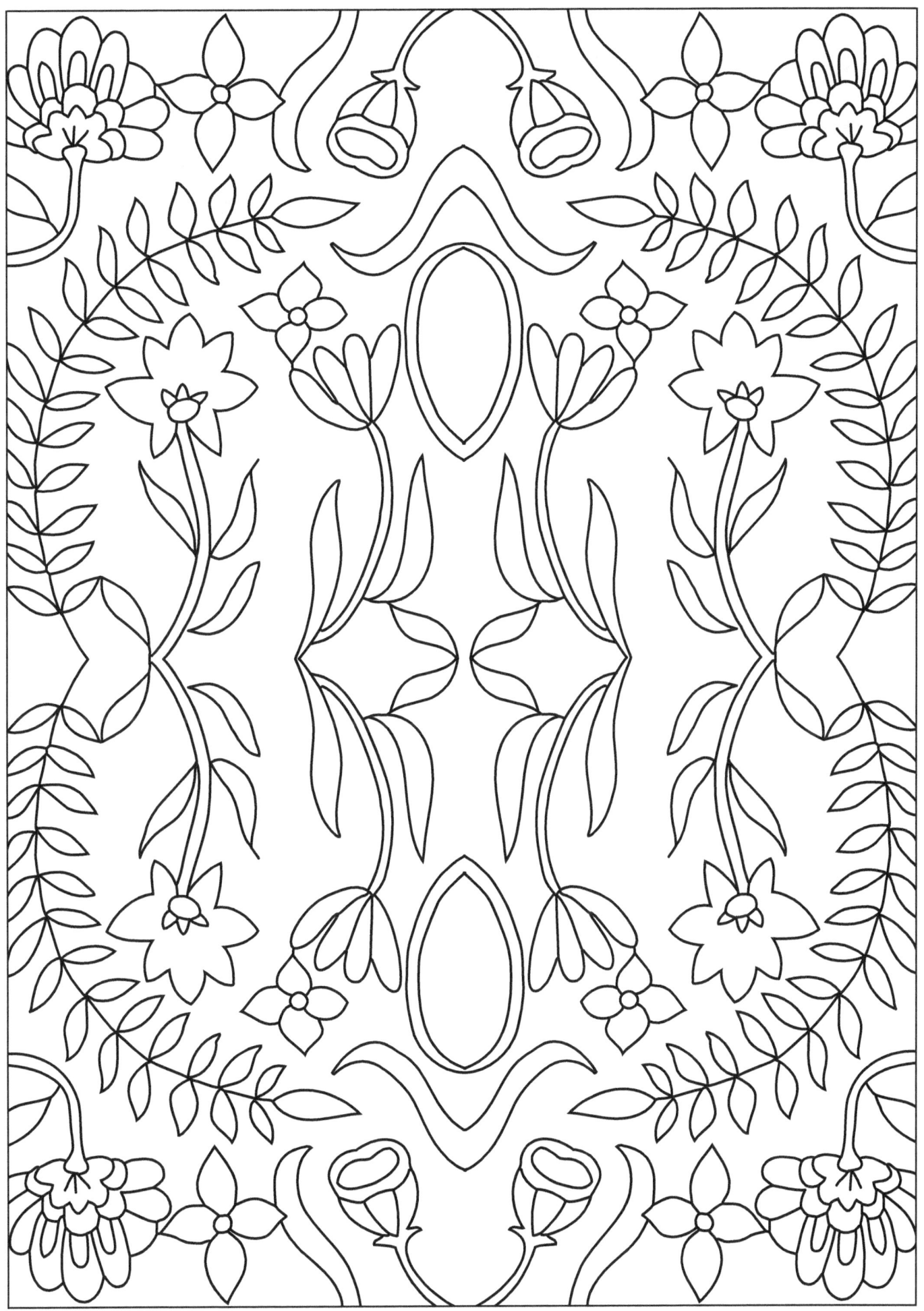

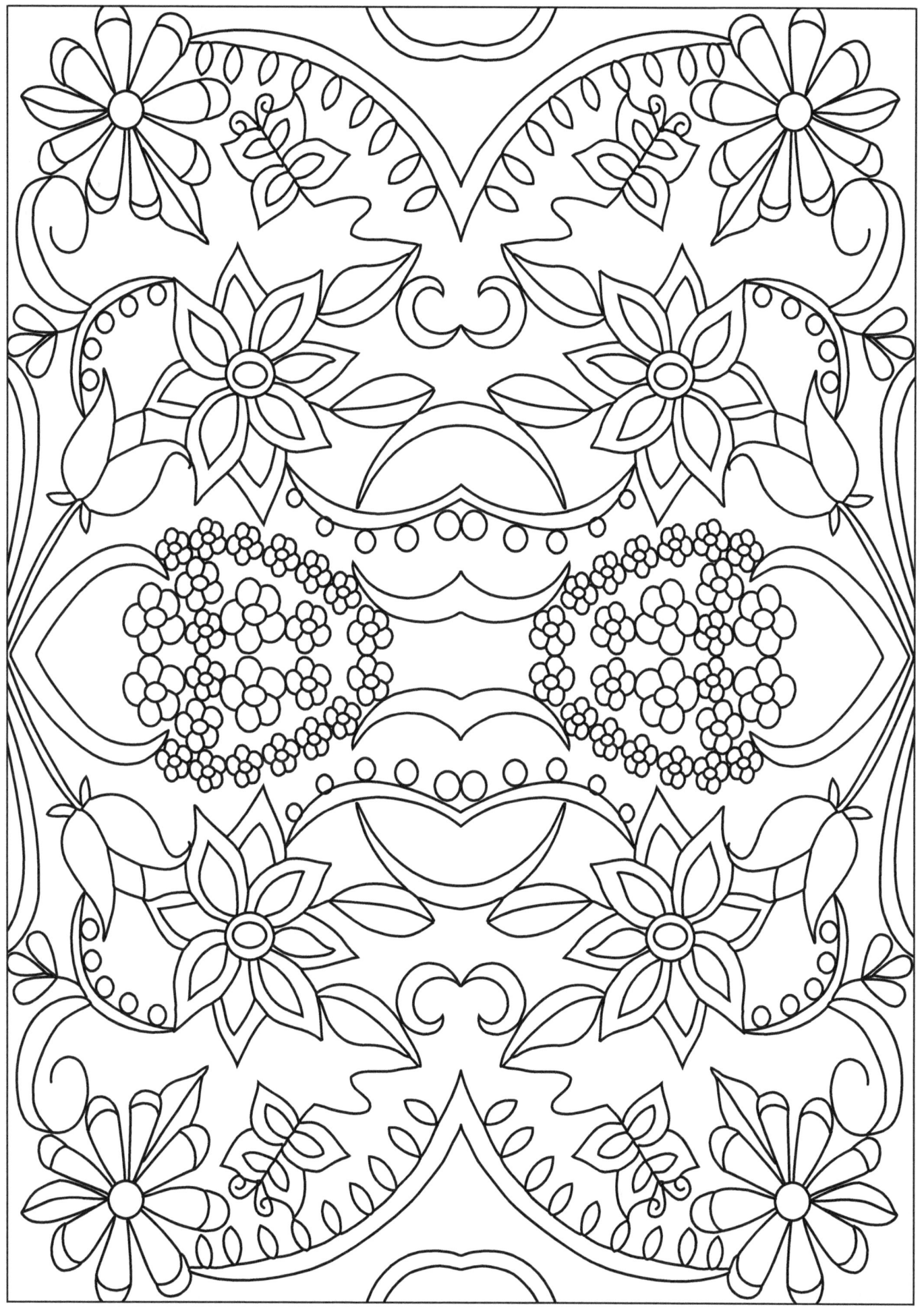

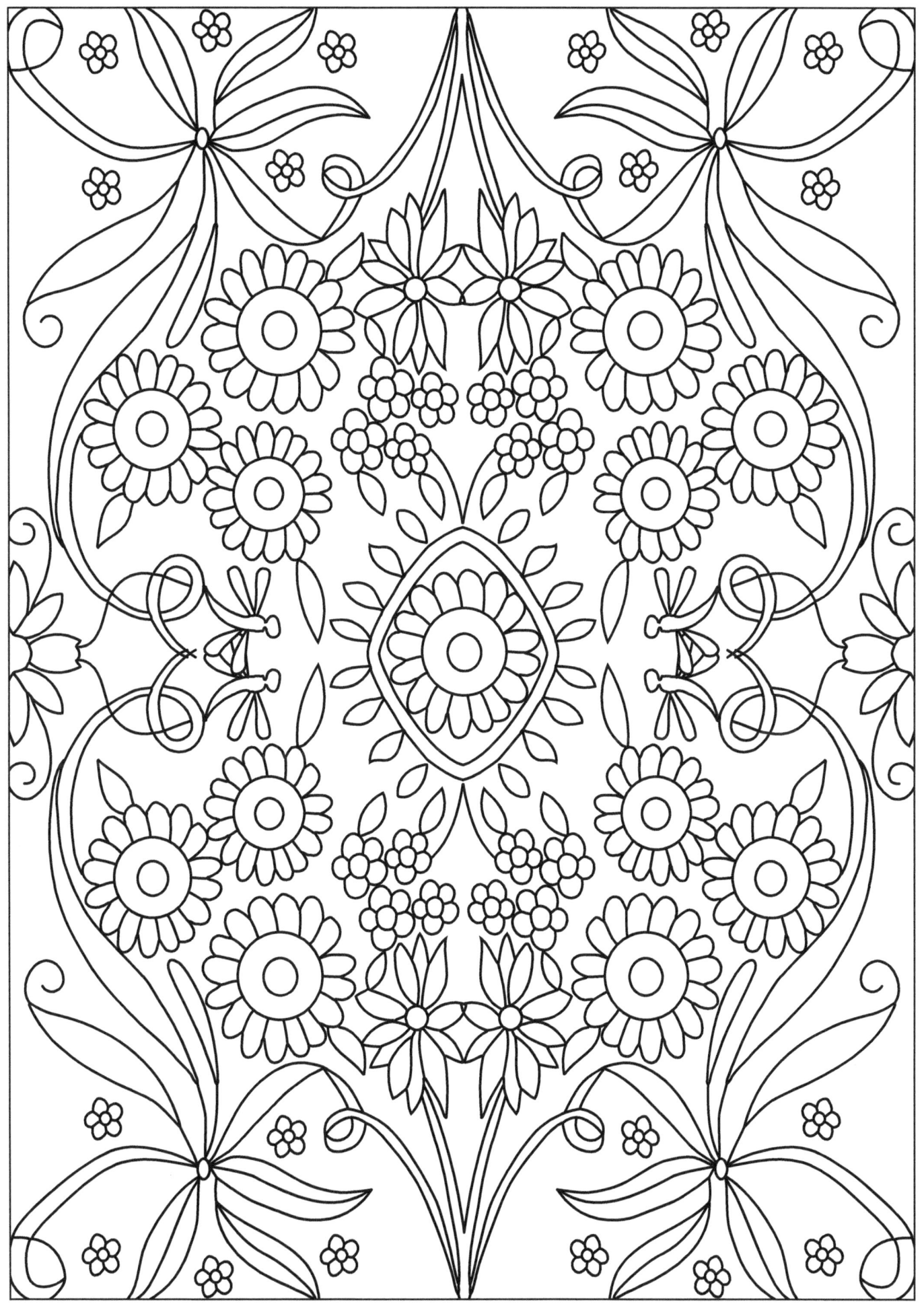

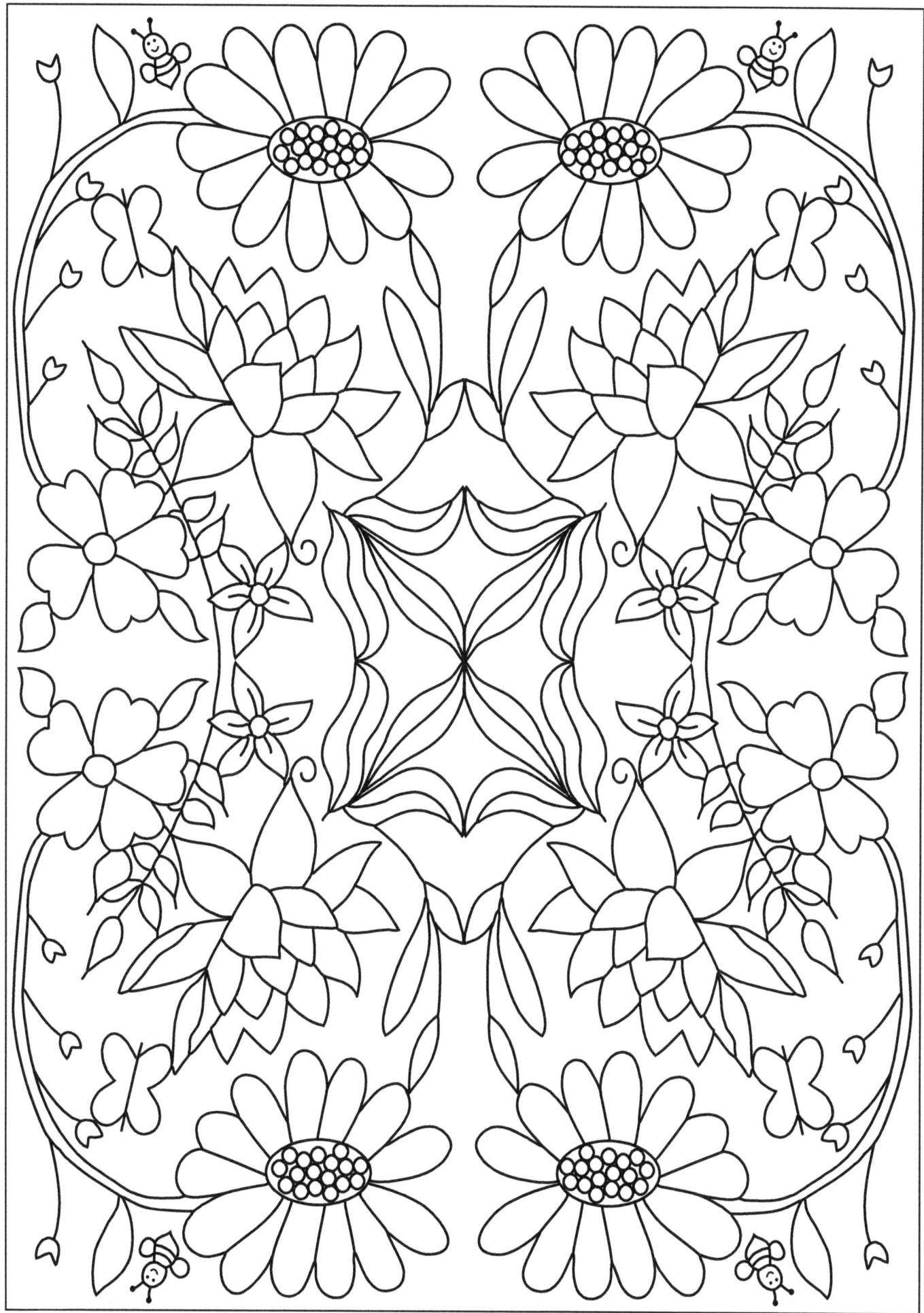

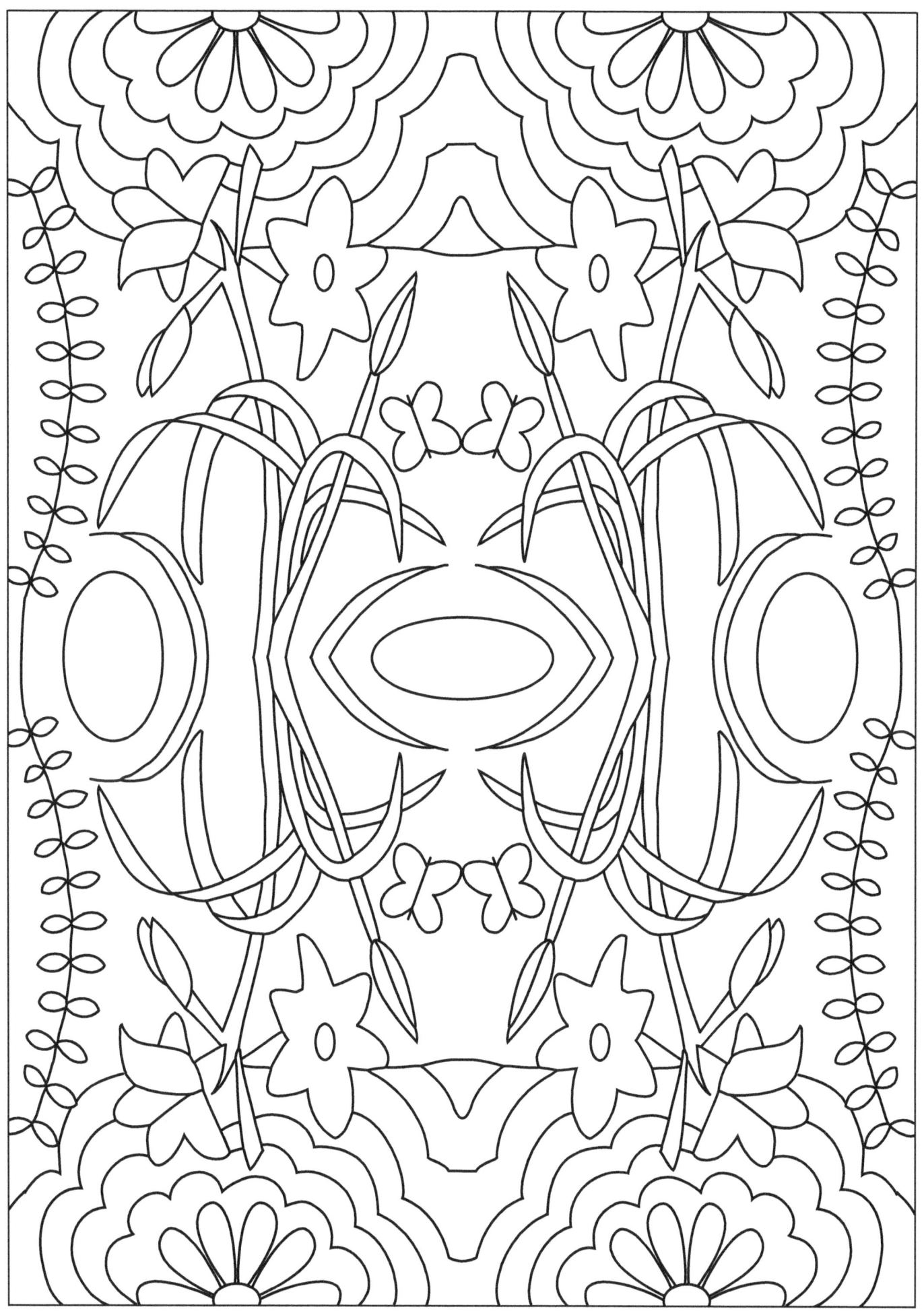

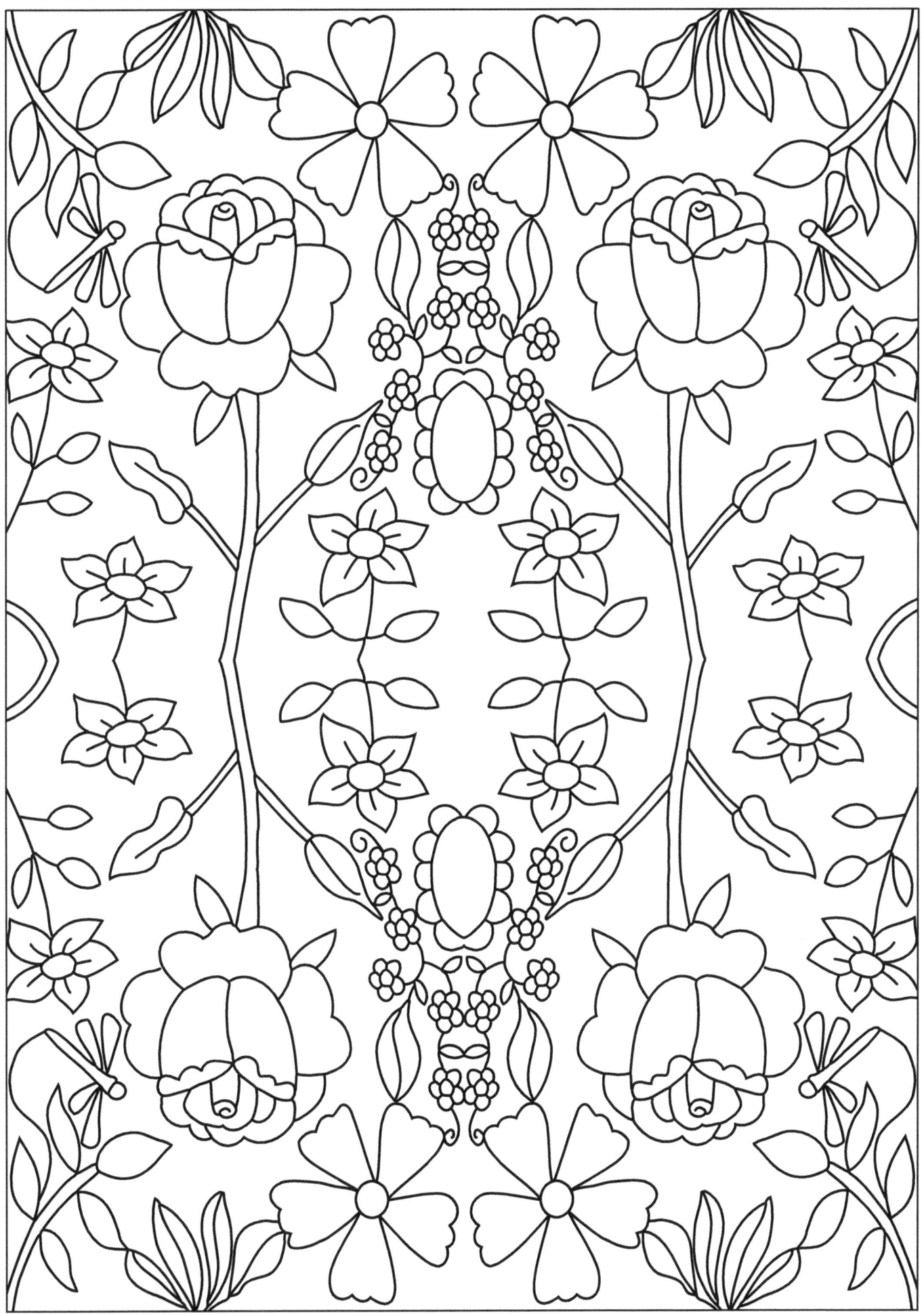

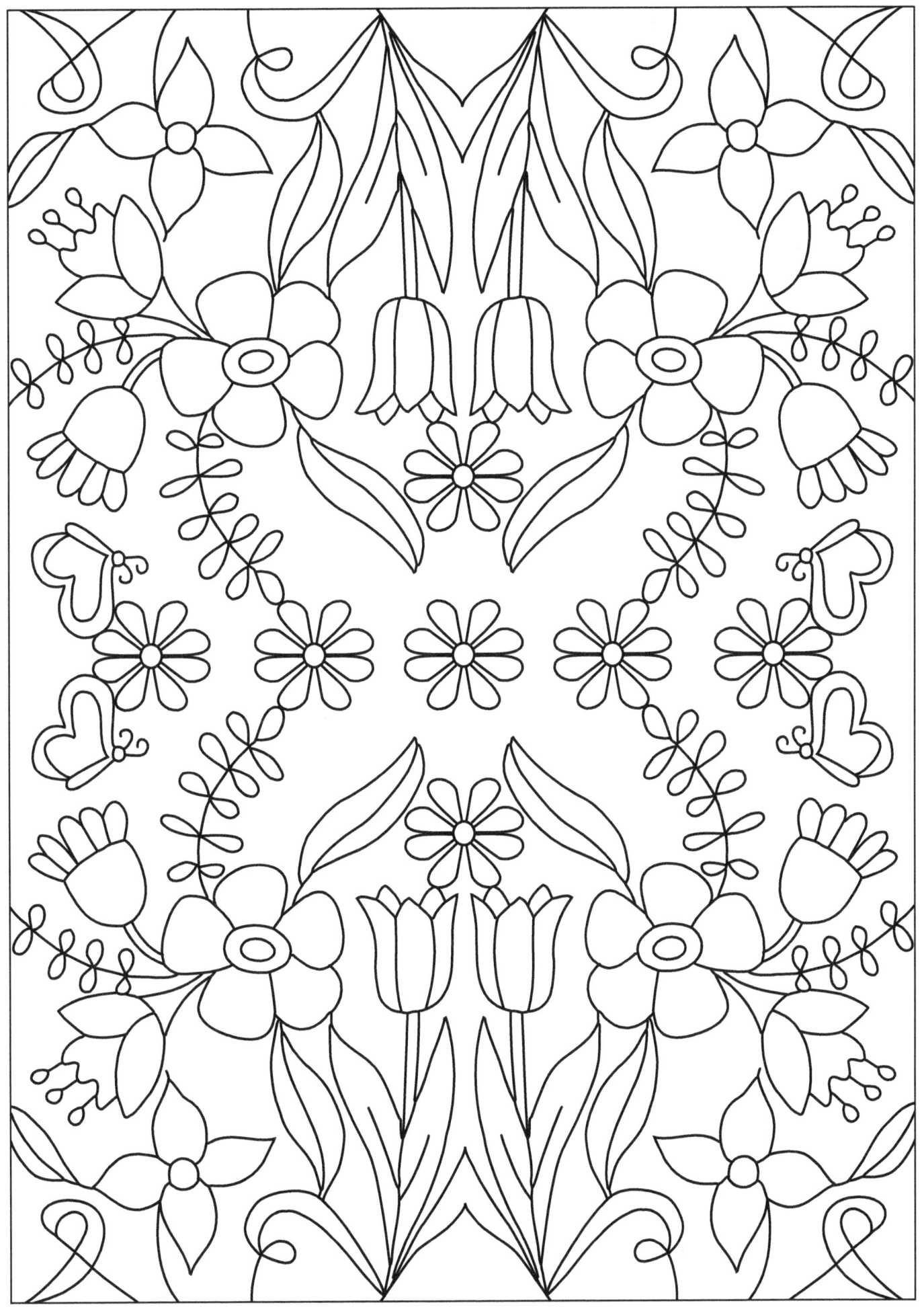

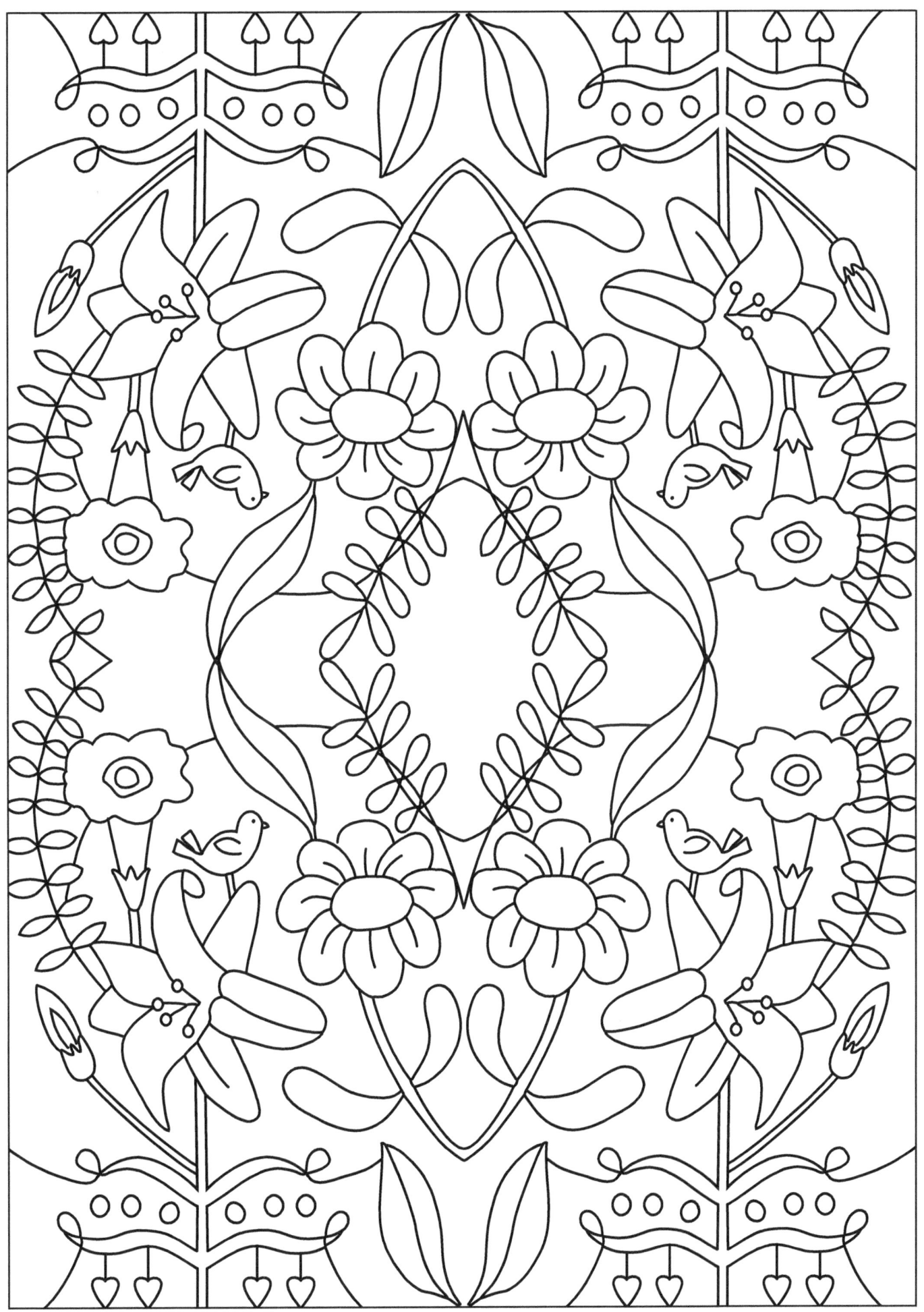

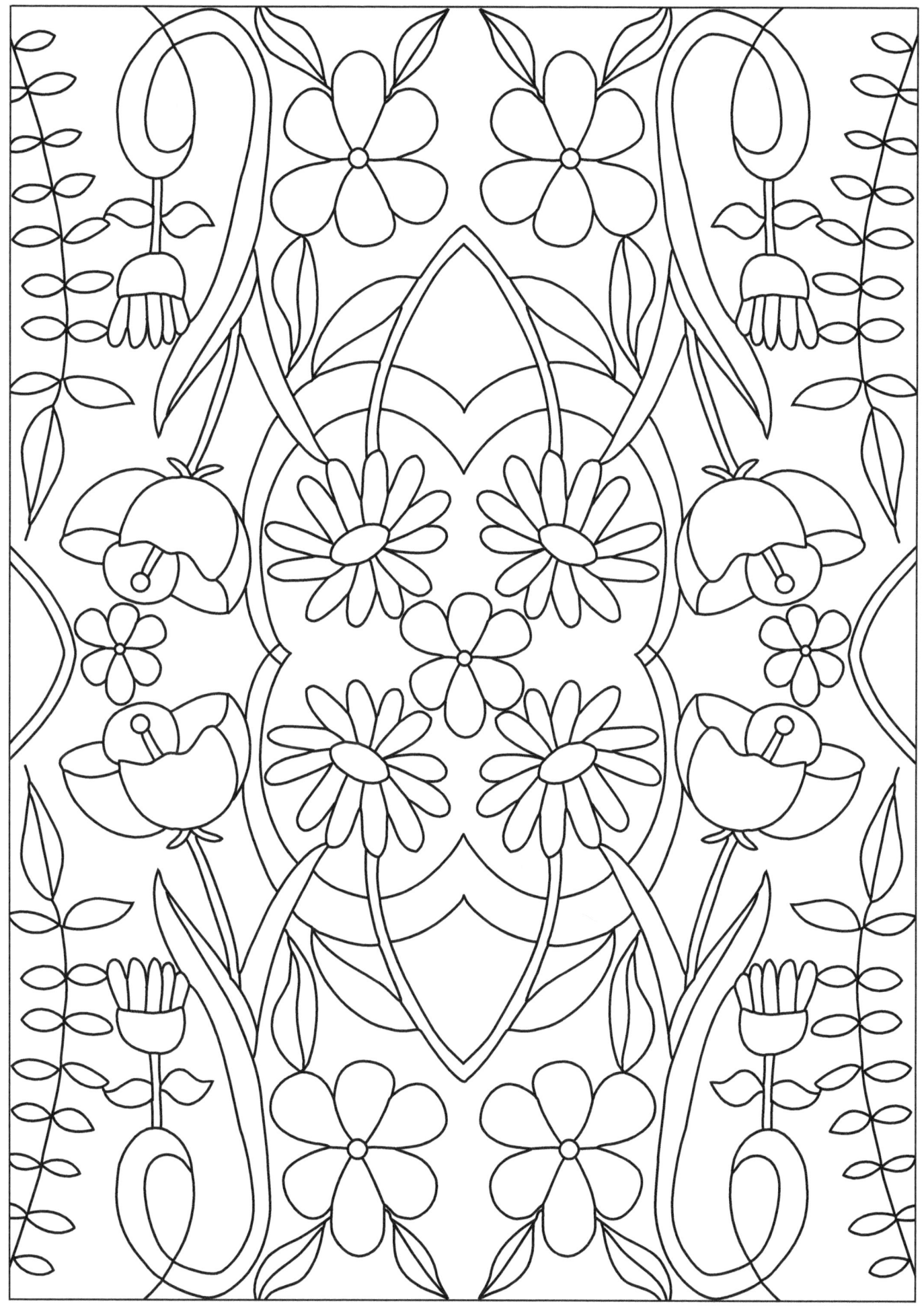

This is your test page. Use this page to test your pencils, crayons etc. Have fun!

www.ingramcontent.com/pod-product-compliance
Lightning Source LLC
Chambersburg PA
CBHW080230180526
45158CB00008BA/2422